A To Z

ONLINE
BOOK PROMOTION TIPS
COLORING BOOK

LASHAUNDA C. HOFFMAN

HOFFMAN CONTENT, LLC

lashaundahoffman.com

This Coloring Book Belongs To

_____

HOFFMAN CONTENT, LLC

lashaundahoffman.com

Printed in the United States of America

First Printing, 2017

ISBN 978-0-9961245-1-5

Hoffman Content LLC
8816 Manchester Rd #231
Brentwood, MO 63144
lchwriter@gmail.com
Sign up for monthly newsletter
www.lashaundahoffman.com

Cover, Interior Design, and Images by Hoffman Content LLC

Ordering Information:
Special discounts are available on quantity purchases by
corporations, associations, and others.
For details, contact the publisher at the address above.

Readers assume all responsibilities for their promotional ventures.

HOFFMAN
CONTENT, LLC
lashaundahoffman.com

Dedicated To

My Gifts From God

Clyde Hoffman

Nichaela Hoffman

Clyde Hoffman Jr.

Sean Hoffman

HOFFMAN CONTENT, LLC

lashaundahoffman.com

Letter From The Author

A few years ago I reawakened my love of coloring. I had so much fun I decided to create my own coloring book.

I wanted to offer something to relieve the stress of promoting.

When promotion stops being fun, pick up this book, color a page, read the assignment on the back and get back to promoting.

Promotion Can Be Fun.
Find the Fun and DO IT!

See Ya On The Net,

LaShaunda
lashaundabooks@gmail.com

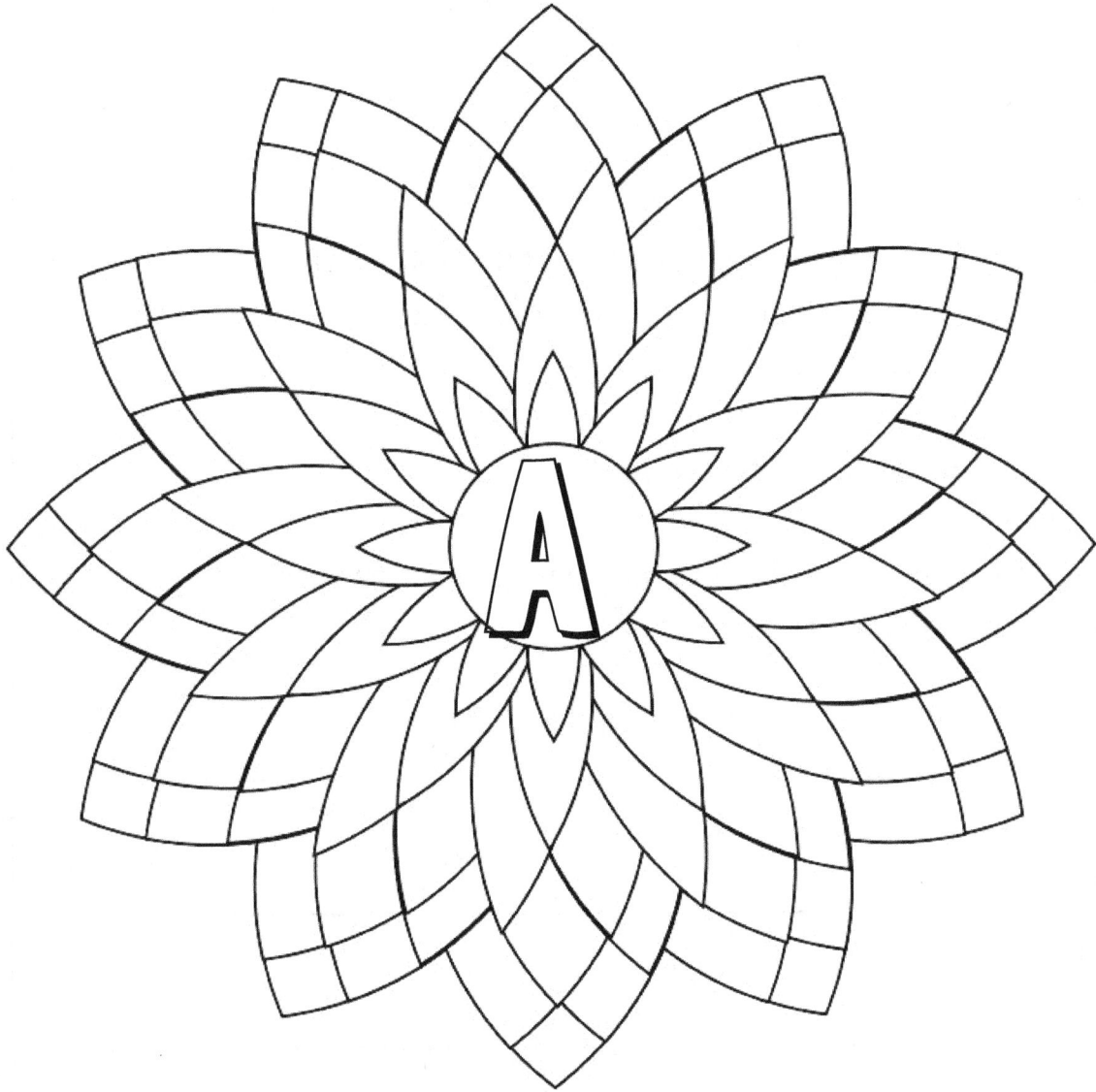

A is for Articles

ARTICLES

Articles are a good way to promote your books. You can discuss a topic you are an expert in and introduce readers to you, your book and your site.

Task

Pick five topics and write five 500 – 800 words articles about these topics. Include a bio, a link to your site and a short blurb about your book.

How to use for promotion

Submit your articles to online magazines or guest blog on different blogs.

_____

_____

_____

_____

_____

B is for Book Clubs

BOOK CLUBS

Looking for a way to meet new readers? Online, book clubs are the way to go. The readers are honest about the books they read and you can ask questions about what they are looking for in a good book.

Task

Join a few online book clubs. Be a member, read the book, participate. Get to know the readers. Don't use it as a place to promote your book. Use it as a way to get to know new readers.

How to use for promotion

Most book clubs often offer their author members a chance to promote their books or use their book as the selection of the month. This is your chance to get some good feedback about your book and hopefully sell a few copies to the members.

_____

_____

_____

_____

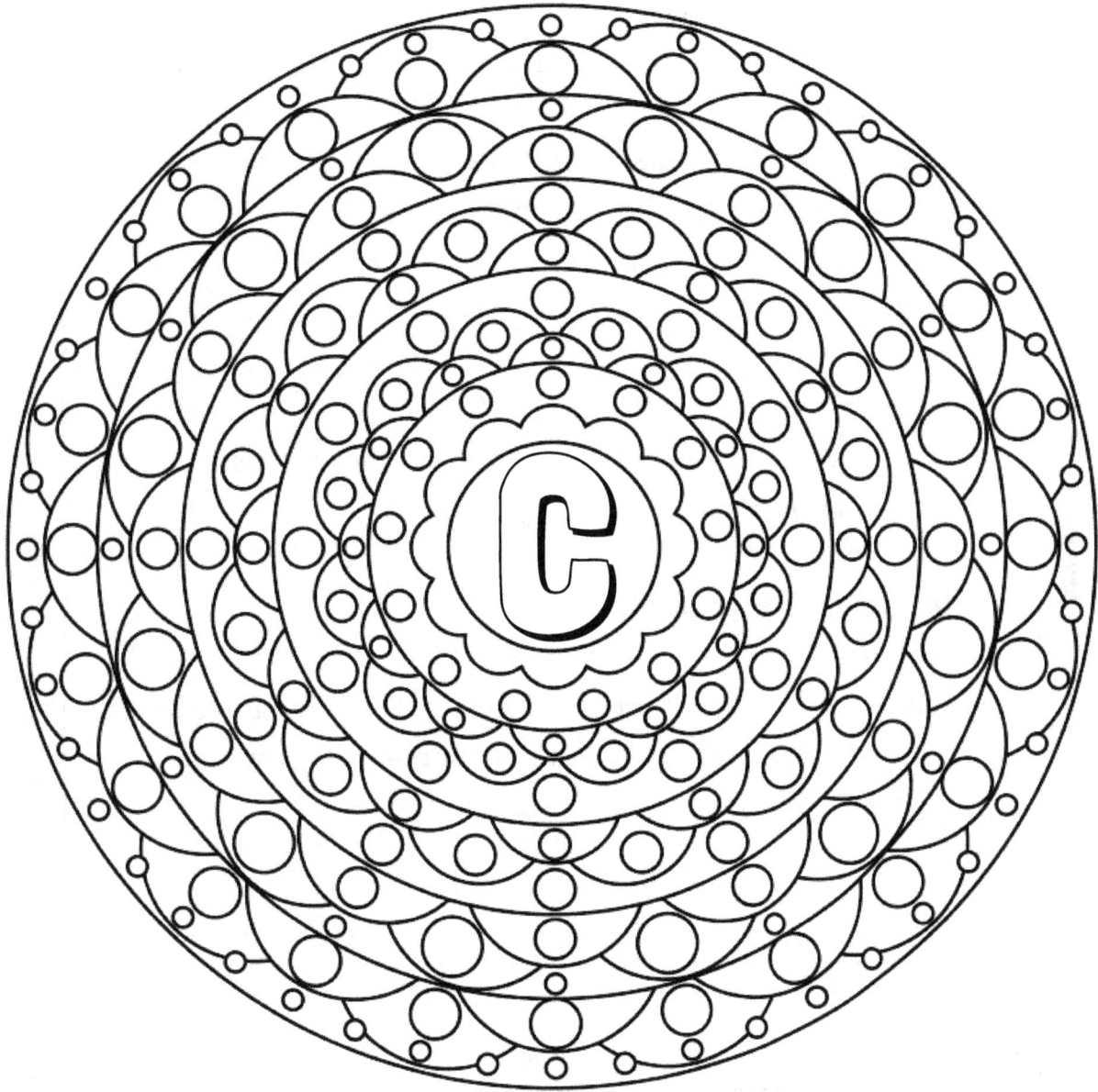

C is for Contact Me

CONTACT ME

You'd be surprised how many writers don't have a
Contact Me page or link to contact on their website. You
are missing out on good promotion opportunities because
there is no way to contact you. Always include a way for
readers, medias and others to contact you.

Task

I suggest you have two contact links, one for your readers
and one for media/others. When you see these messages,
you will know exactly who they are from.

How to use for promotion

Include a contact form or email link on your site. Readers
can send you a message through your contact form or a
magazine can contact you for an interview.

_____

_____

_____

_____

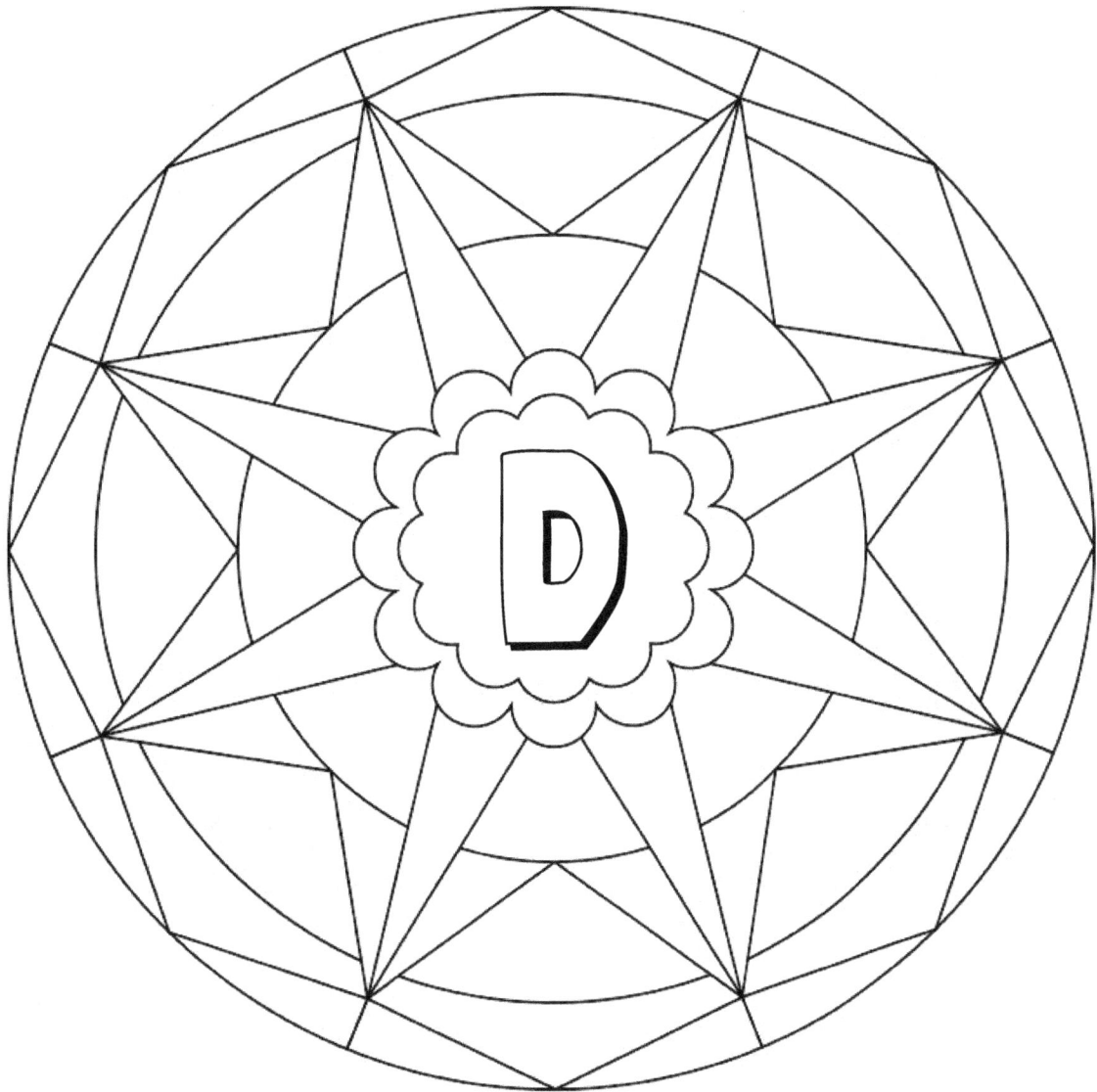

D is for Daily

DAILY

Most writers think they don't have time for daily promotion. However if you take time to schedule your promotion, you can have promotions going out every day and it looks like you are a busy little writer.

Task

Pick one day to schedule your daily posts. Use Hootsuites or Buffer to do bulk scheduling.

How to use for promotion

Scheduling keeps you consistent with your promotion. It's great for days you don't have time to promote. Your promotion is going out and you can find time to do other tasks.

_____

_____

_____

_____

_____

E is for Email Signature

EMAIL SIGNATURE

This is one of the cheapest ways you can market your book, and it's the best way to talk about your book without saying a word. You can change it up weekly or monthly.

What is a signature?

A signature is a mini bio. I've seen some introduce the author, some introduce a book, and some introduce a site. Only you can determine what you want on your signature.

Task

Create a signature

Name
Title of Book
Date of release (or 25 words or less blurb)
Website link
If you can, add a little color and hyperlink to your site, so the reader can click on and see your book or site.

How to use for promotion

This is the perfect way to introduce your book to whoever reads your email.
You can use it to announce the book release.
You can use it to announce your latest contest.
You can include a link to an excerpt.

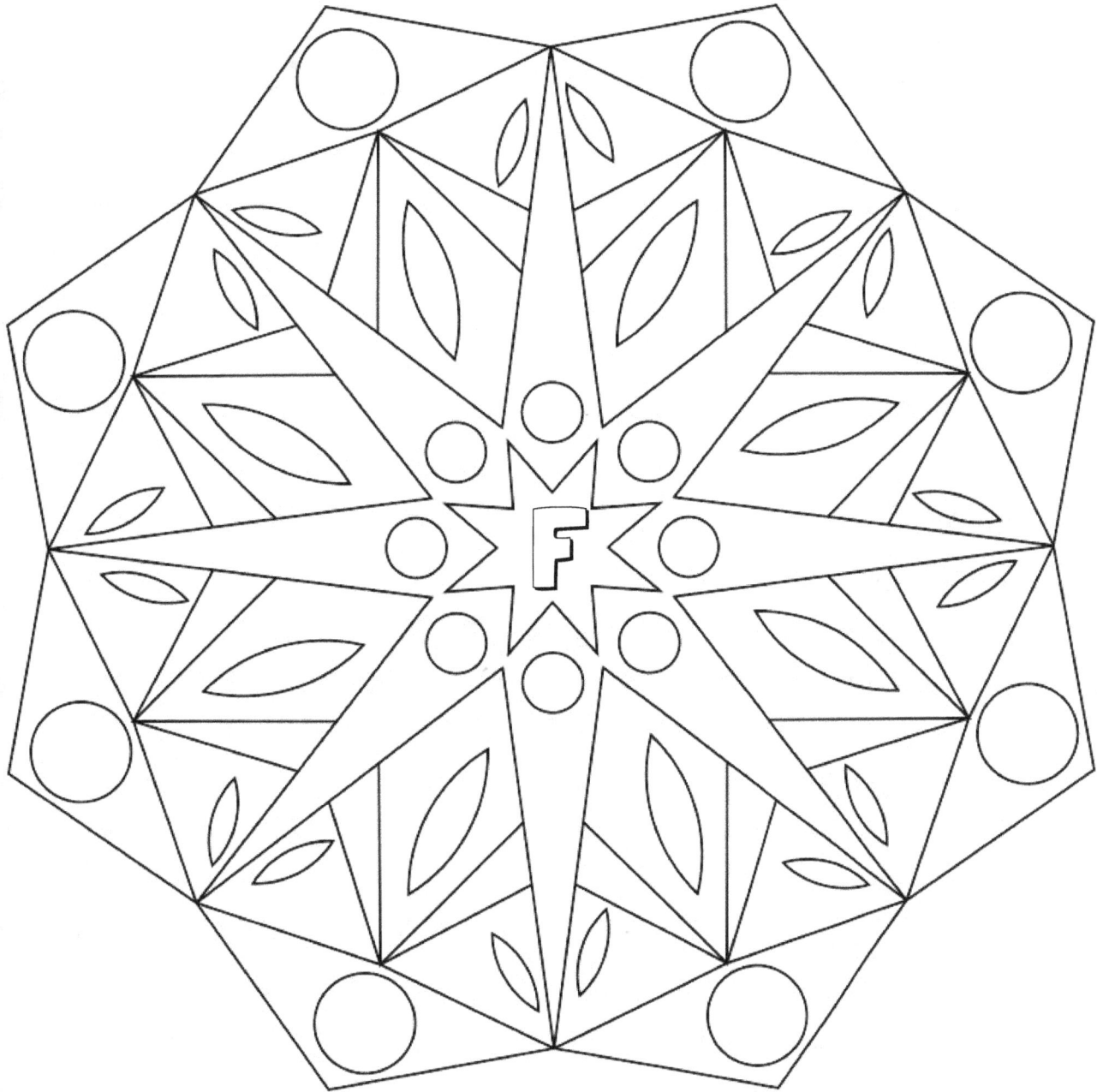

F is for Facebook

FACEBOOK

Facebook is a good platform for building relationships with readers.

Task

Chat with five followers each day.
Write five questions to ask your followers.
Share someone's content everyday.

How To Use For Promotion

Take time to interact with your readers. This is your chance to get to know your readers. Use them for your book research, show them excerpts of your book, ask them questions about what they like and don't like about your books.

_____

_____

_____

_____

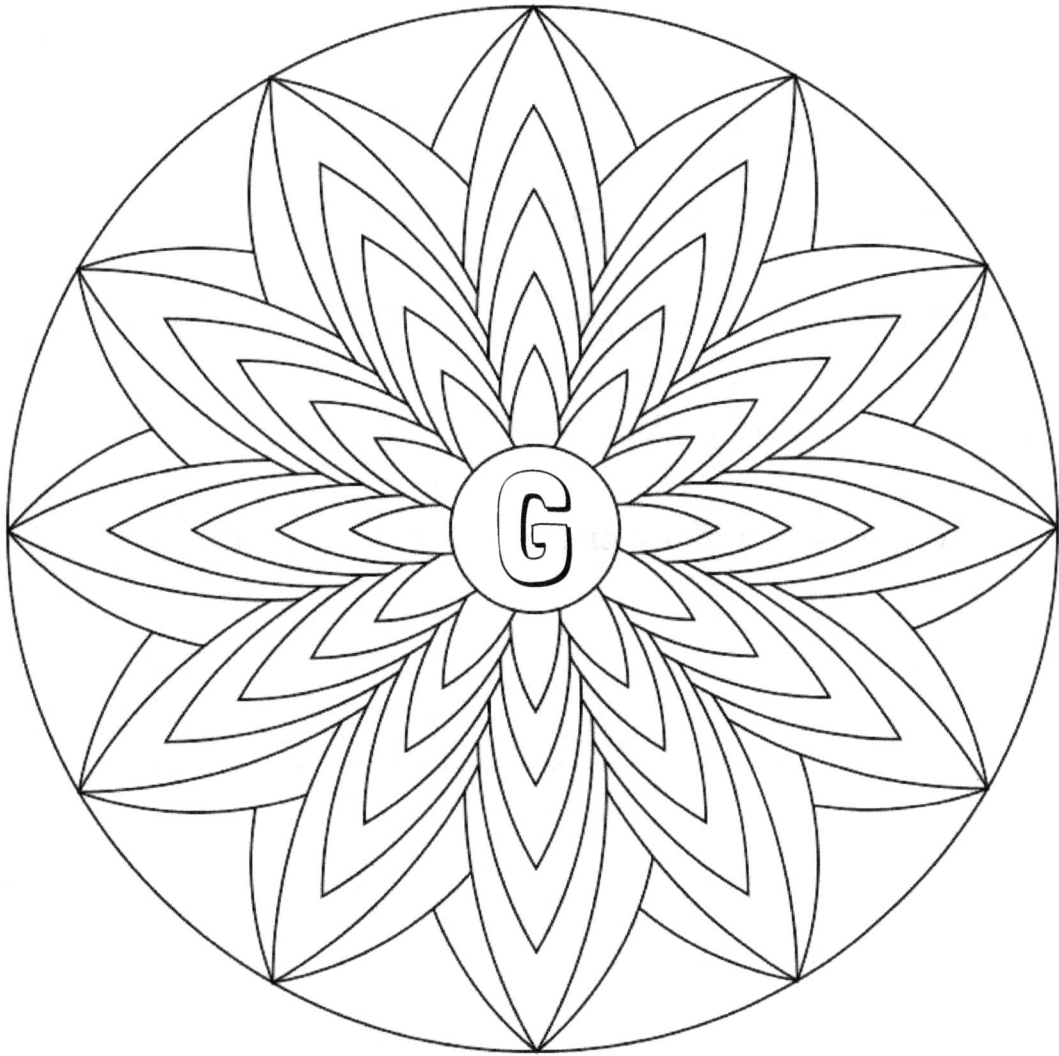

G is for Groups

GROUPS

Groups are a good way to meet new readers. Most platforms have groups you can join and participate in.

Task

Find five groups that focus on the genres you write.

How To Use For Promotion

Groups are the perfect place to showcase your expertise. You can be the featured author or you can have a book discussion. You can ask the group members advice on an excerpt, or for feedback on a work in progress.

_____

_____

_____

_____

_____

H

H is for Hootsuite

HOOTSUITE

Hootsuite.com has become one of my favorite tools when it comes to promotion. I use it for scheduling my promotion and I also use it to check out what's going on with my different social media platforms.

I like being able to look at all the social media platforms on one page vs opening up different windows. I like that I can share content right there. If you like to retweet on Twitter, it gives you the opportunity to do so.

Looking for new content, Hootsuite lets you look through your platforms for content to share.

Task

Hootsuite, offers a free version, so you can check it out. I signed up for the paid service, so I could add my FB pages and groups to it. It's been worth the money for me.

How to use for promotion

Schedule your promotion. Find content you can schedule for later. Retweet content you find interesting. Chat with your followers on different platforms.

I

I is for Interviews

INTERVIEWS

An interview is a fun way to promote your book and meet new readers. Take time to schedule one or two interviews a month.

Below are a few tips to help with your interviews.

1. Complete the interview.

2. Copy and paste the interview.

3. Include a picture.

4. Include an email address or contact info.

5. Return the interview on time.

6. Visit the site/blog featuring your interview.

7. Offer an autographed book or prize for a lucky winner.

8. Send out an announcement to your mailing list, newsletter, and social media.

9. Include a link on your site.

10. Send a thank you note/email.

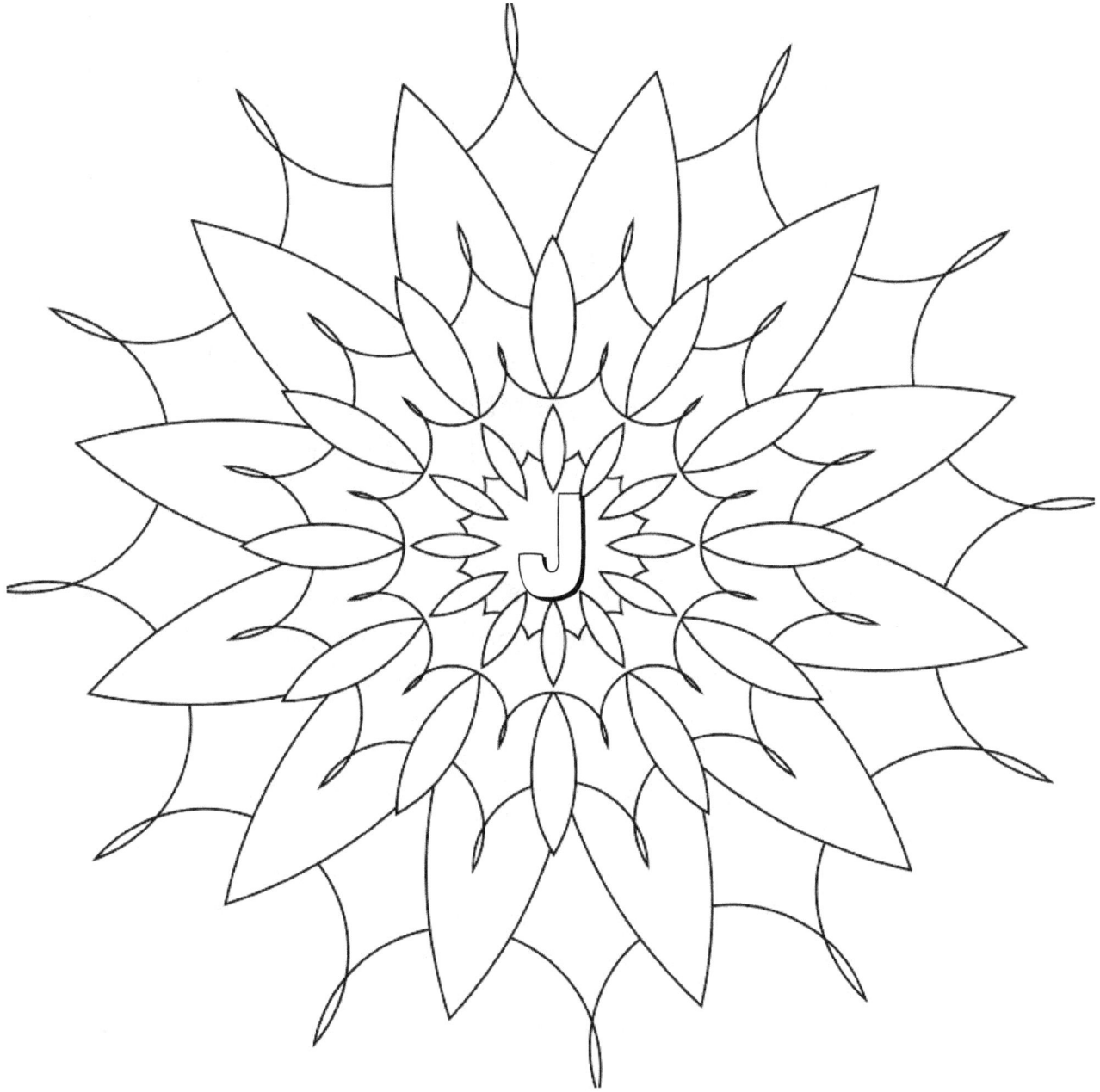

J is for Jargon

JARGON

When you start promoting your books, there are a few jargons that come up a lot. Here are a few:

Blurb – A short summary of your book that is normally used for the text on the back cover.

Synopsis – A summary of the major points of your book. It's usually a bit longer than the blurb. Sometimes they can be one or two pages or to 25 pages depending on who is requesting it.

ARC - Advance Reading Copy, an uncorrected proof, or bound galley proof of a manuscript that is sent out to book reviewers.

Genre - A category of literary works (romance, mystery, historical, suspense, etc.).

Theme - The main subject that is being discussed or described in a piece of writing.

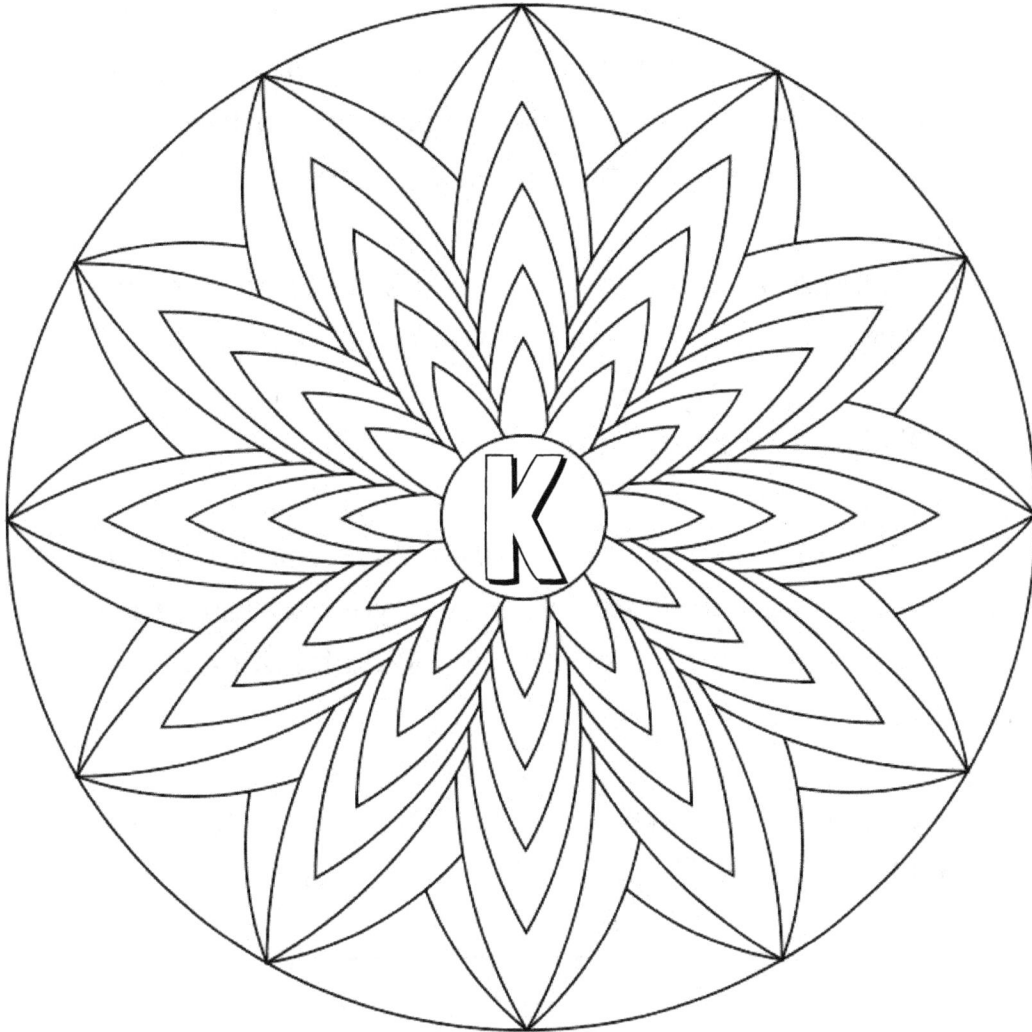

K is for Keep

KEEP

Keep A Calendar

When it comes to promotion consistency is very important. I recommend to my clients to keep a calendar. It will help you to remain consistent. Using a social media manager like Hootsuite is also another way to keep you consistent.

When your promotion is sporadic, you let other things get in your way and before you know it you're not promoting.

How To Use For Promotion

Create a promotion calendar. It will include your social media schedule, your schedule for live events, your schedule for interviews and all the things you plan to do for your promotion.

Then stick to it daily. When those book sells start coming in, you will be happy you stayed consistent.

_____

_____

_____

_____

L is for Letters

LETTERS

Letters of introduction are the best ways to pitch yourself to an online magazine, radio show, or podcasts. Here are a few tips to help you create a letter that will be answered.

Do your research - Is this the place you want to be promoted on? Do they promote your type of books? What are their guidelines?

*You don't want to introduce yourself to a site that only features non-fiction when you write romance. Don't waste their time or yours.

Read their guidelines - How do they want you to submit to their site? How soon can you be featured on their site?

*This is important because some sites have strict guidelines. Don't think you will get your book featured the week it comes out when you send them the introduction letter the week it comes out.

Make sure you have the right person to submit to

You want to make sure you are addressing your letter to the right person. This is why you do your research.

* Nothing gets a letter deleted faster than the wrong name. I will forgive LaShaundra instead of LaShaunda, however the next person might not. Get the name and title right.

M is for Mailing List

MAILING LIST

Three Ways To Use Your Mailing List

1. Monthly Newsletter

Showcase a reader
Host a contest

2. Announcements

Cover Reveal
Events you'll be attending

3. Sales

Create eblasts for monthly sales
Host workshops

_____

_____

_____

_____

N

N is for Newsletters

NEWSLETTERS

Newsletters are a good way to communicate with your readers. You can keep them up to date with what's going on with your writing and books.

Task: Invite your social media followers to subscribe to your newsletter.

Schedule the invite to go out weekly.

How to use for promotion

You can feature your upcoming events dates.
You can do mini interviews with fellow authors.
You can showcase pictures of events you attended.
You can offer writing tips.
You can answer fan letters.
Make your newsletter fun and keep a subscribe link on your website.

_____

_____

_____

_____

_____

O

O is for Online Conference

ONLINE CONFERENCE

Here are five ways to get the most out of an online conference:

1. **Participate** – Join in on the discussions, share your wisdom, meet new people, have a little fun. There is always a chance to introduce yourself and your book. Take advantage of this and toot your own horn.

2. **Links** – Make sure you include a link to your website with every post. You want those in attendance to stop by your website. They can't visit if you don't share your website address.

3. **Invite** – Do you have an email list or newsletter? Invite the attendees to sign up for your newsletter.

4. **Donate** – Make donations to the conference. Attendees love winning prizes. Guess who they will be talking about if they win your fabulous prize?

5. **Sponsorship** – Become a sponsor. Most sponsorships consist of some sort of advertisement. This is a great way to stay in front of the attendees, because they have a program they keep with your information in it.

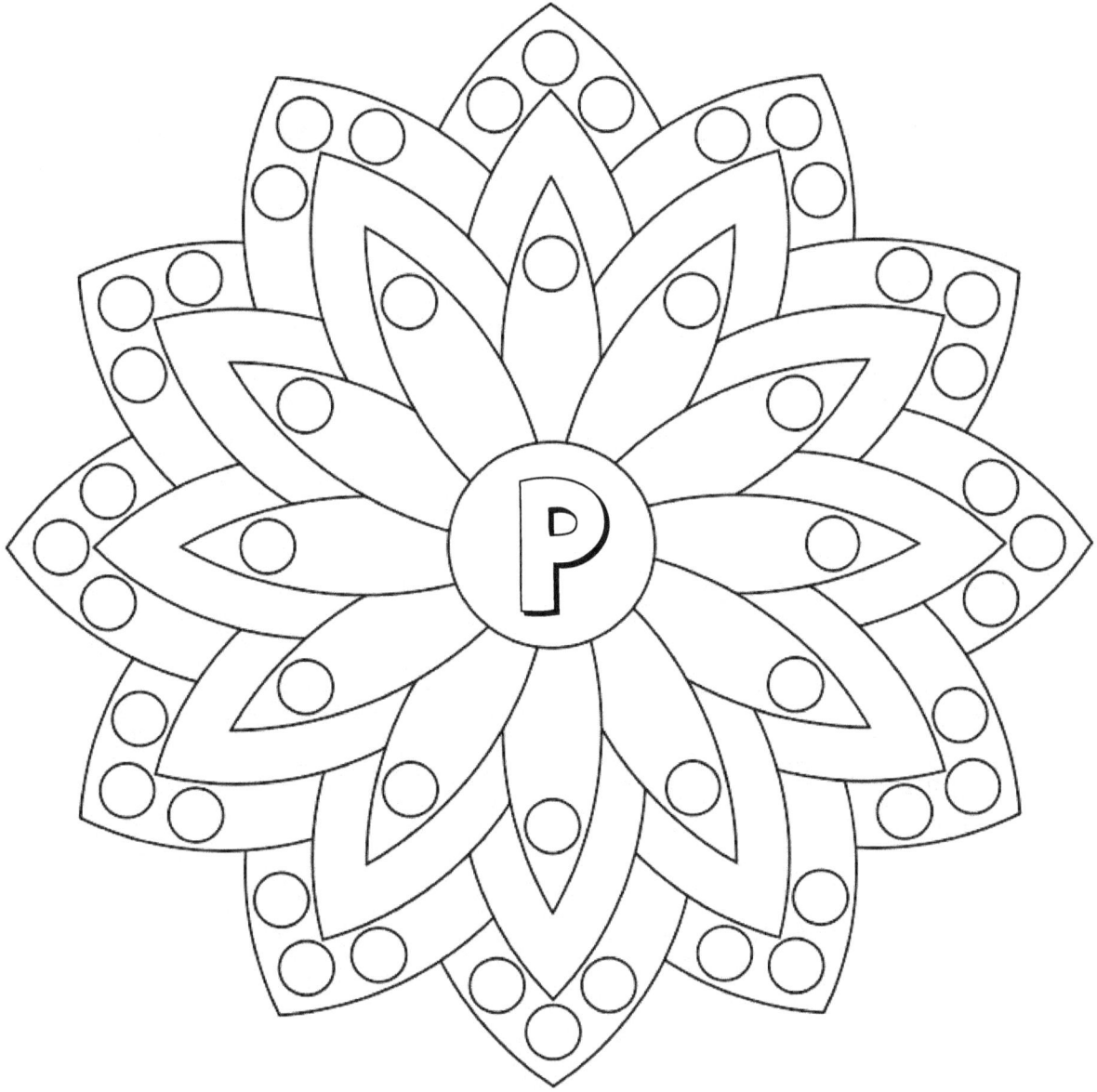

P is for Promotion Plan

PROMOTION PLAN

Your promotion plan is all about how you are getting in front of the readers. It also keeps you consistent with your promotion.

Your plan includes:

1. **Promotion goals** – what do you want to do?

2. **A promotion budget** – how much do you plan on spending?

3. **A promotion schedule** – how often will you promote and where?

4. **Promotion content** – what you will you promote?

5. **Your results goals** – the results of your promotion (sells, new subscribers, new followers, invites, etc).

Q is for Questions

QUESTIONS

Most writers don't ask questions when it comes to their promotions, so they don't get the help they need to get their books out there.

Do you accept indie books for review?

How much does it cost to feature my book in your magazine?

How do I set up a mailing list?

How do I use a social media manager?

Don't be afraid to ask questions when it comes to your promotion.

What are your promotion questions?

_____

_____

_____

_____

_____

_____

R is for Readers

READERS

Know who your reader is.

Most writers don't think about their readers when they start writing their books. However, this is the perfect time to imagine who will be reading your books. You want to cater your writing to this reader. You want to be able to touch deep inside of their hearts.

Answer the following questions about your reader?

What age is your reader?

What is your reader's gender?

Where does your reader live?

How much does your reader make?

What is your reader's education level?

What is your reader's marital status?

What type of lifestyle does your reader have?

How often does your reader read books?

How often does your reader buy books?

What is your reader's guilty pleasures?

Does your reader resemble what you had in your mind?

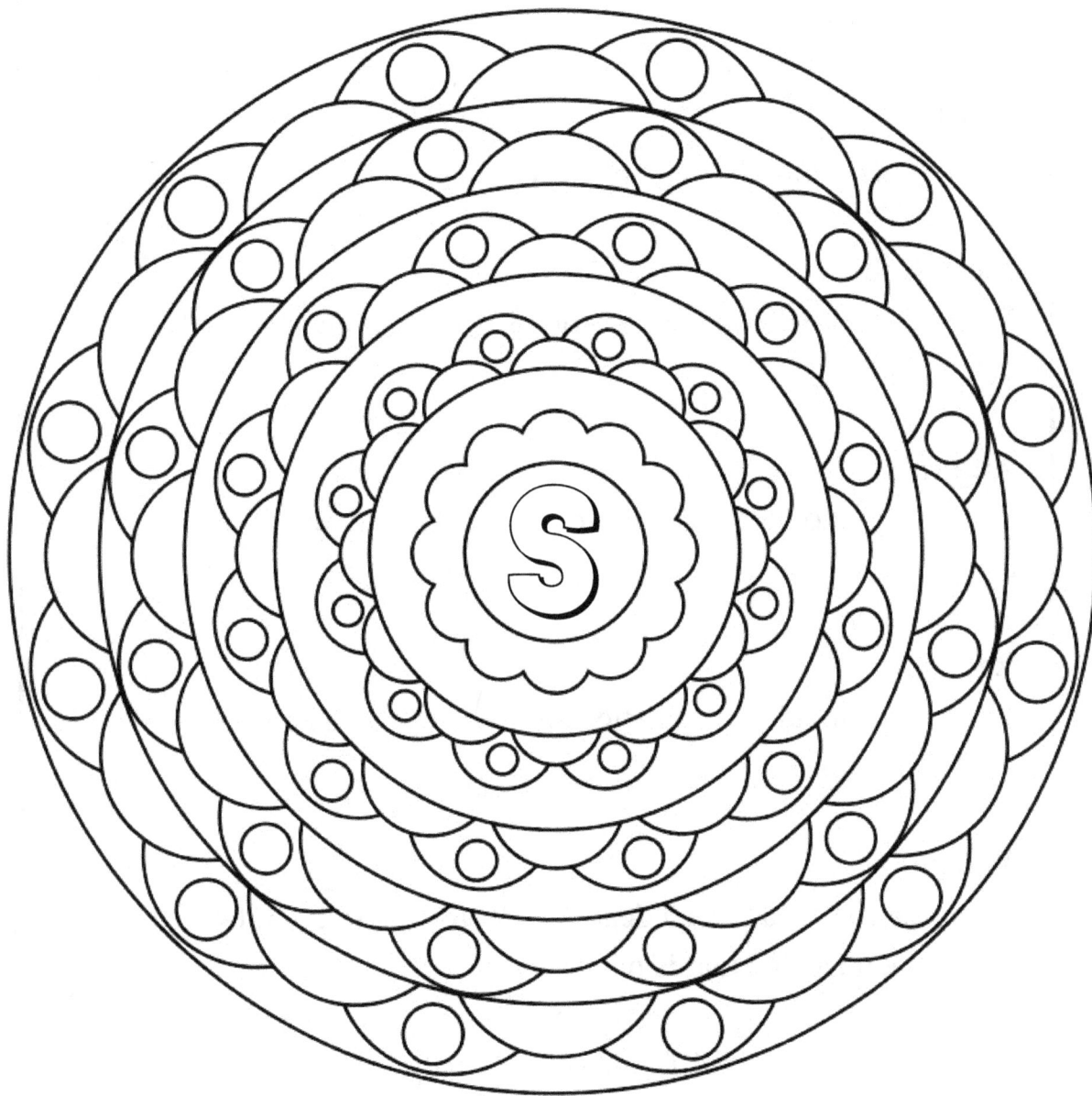

S is for Smart Goals

SMART GOALS

Do you set SMART Goals?

What are SMART Goals? SMART is a term created by George T. Doran that stands for:

Specific
Your goals should be very specific.

Measurable
Your goals should be measurable. So you know when you've reached them.

Attainable
Your goals should be attainable. Don't set goals you'll never reach.

Realistic
Your goals should be realistic, something you can complete and you have control over.

Timely
Your goals should have a deadline. You want to complete your goals, not have one that is never ending.

As a writer you have different sets of goals:
Personal Goals
Writing Goals
Marketing Goals
Business Goals
Schedule some time to work on your goals.

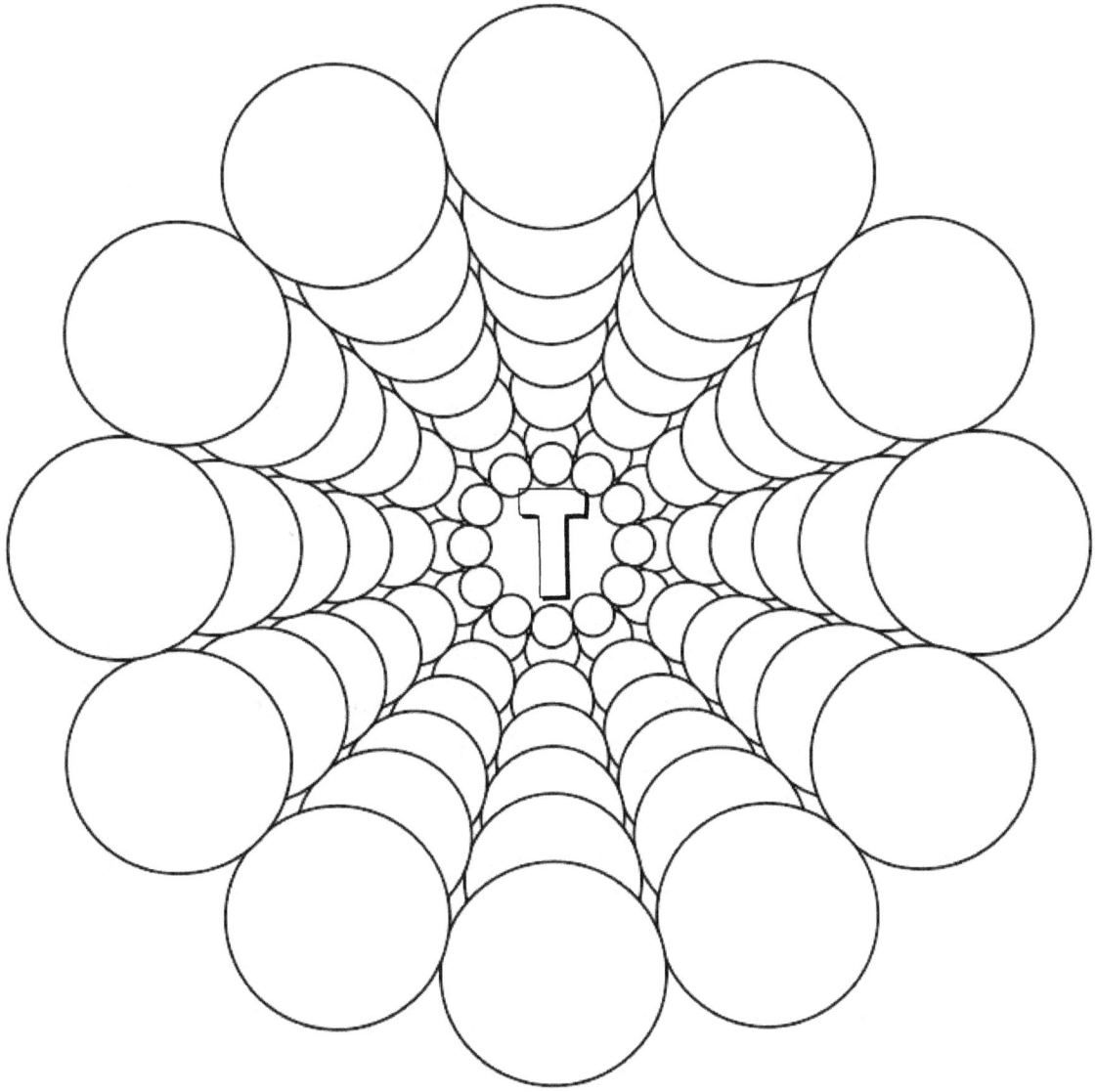

T is for Tours

TOURS - Blog Tours

Blog tours introduce you to the blog readers. Most authors do it wrong because they are thinking of sells versus meeting new readers. Your goal for the blog tour should be to interact with as many readers as you can. That's why you want an interactive blog tour, not one that just posts information. You want to communicate with the blog's readers. You want them to get to know you and be interested in you, so they will come back to your website and join your community.

Blog Tour Tips

1. Schedule a blog tour when you have time to give it your complete attention. One week is better than two weeks or a month. Don't schedule one when you are on deadline. A blog tour will only become added stress.

2. Check out other blog tours and see what you like about them and incorporate those features into your tour. You want to make the tour fun, something you want to do - not have to do.

3. Schedule your time to visit each site at least once a day. Two times a day is even better.

4. Schedule your blog tour on your calendar. Tell everybody you know about your blog tour schedule. Post it on your website and social medias. Be excited to meet new readers.

5. Create goals for this blog tour: How many new readers would you like to add to your mailing list? How many reviews would you like to get from this blog tour? How many new contacts?

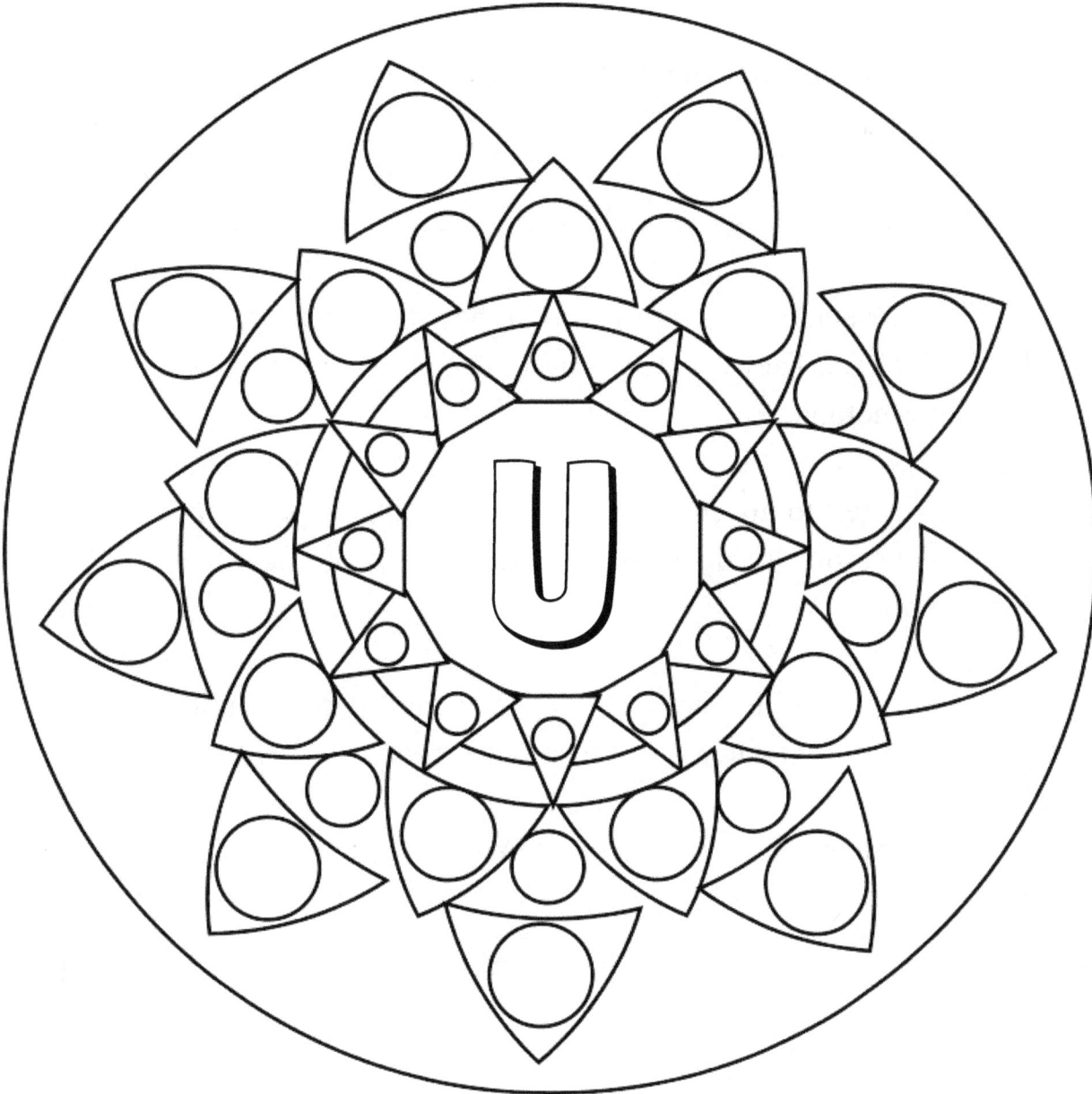

U is for Understand

UNDERSTAND

Understand that you don't have to master every social media platform.

Find which works well for you and use that platform.

Many authors think they have to be on every social media platform. They eventually become overwhelmed and stop promoting.

I suggest to my clients they should pick three platforms and participate on them. Have fun and it won't feel like work.

Don't try to master everything. Become an expert in three platforms and interact with your readers.

What are your favorite platforms?:

_____

_____

_____

_____

V

V is for Video

VIDEO

Did you know the biggest search engine is YouTube?
People are using it to learn how to do things, to share their
content, and to reach new readers.

Have you joined the fun?

Task

Do you have a YouTube channel?

Share the link to your community?

How to use for promotion

Create videos on how to write.
Read excerpts of your books.
Interview your writer friends.

_____

_____

_____

_____

W is for Why

WHY?

This is a question most writers don't think about. Most are on social media because that's what THEY say to do. However, when you join a social media platform you need to know WHY?

Knowing why you are on social media will help you determine your goals for social media, then you can create a plan to help you find time to be on social media, get results from being on social media, and feel like you're getting something out of social media.

Answer the following questions:

Why are you on social media?
What do you want to gain from social media?
How often do you think you should be on social media?
What do you like and dislike about social media?
What will you share on social media?
What social media platforms do you like?

Look over your answers and determine

How often you want to be on social media.
What you will share on social media.
What social media platforms will you be on.
Will you create a social media calendar.

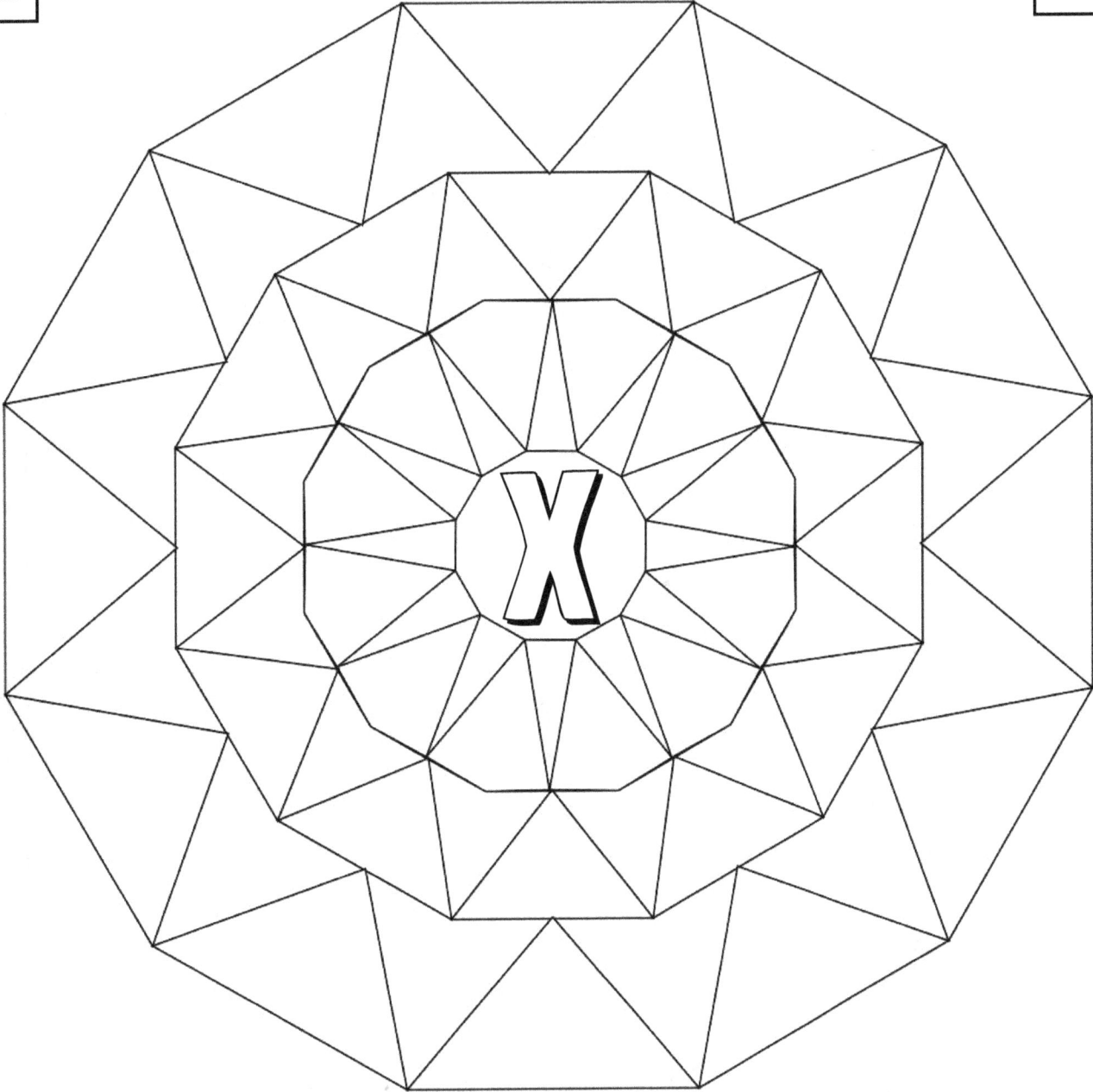

X

X is for Xenial

Xenial

Xenial means "friendly relationship between host and guest."

Building relationship is always important when it comes to promotion.

You start building relationships by becoming a social butterfly.

A social butterfly isn't about "buy my book," they are about offering good content people come back to read.

A social butterfly will respond to comments and questions and not leave their followers hanging.

A social butterfly will share other people's content, because they believe in sharing things of value.

A social butterfly is always thinking of ways to build relationships with their followers.

Are you a social butterfly or a fly lurking on the wall?

Showcase your beautiful butterfly wings daily and you will begin to build relationships.

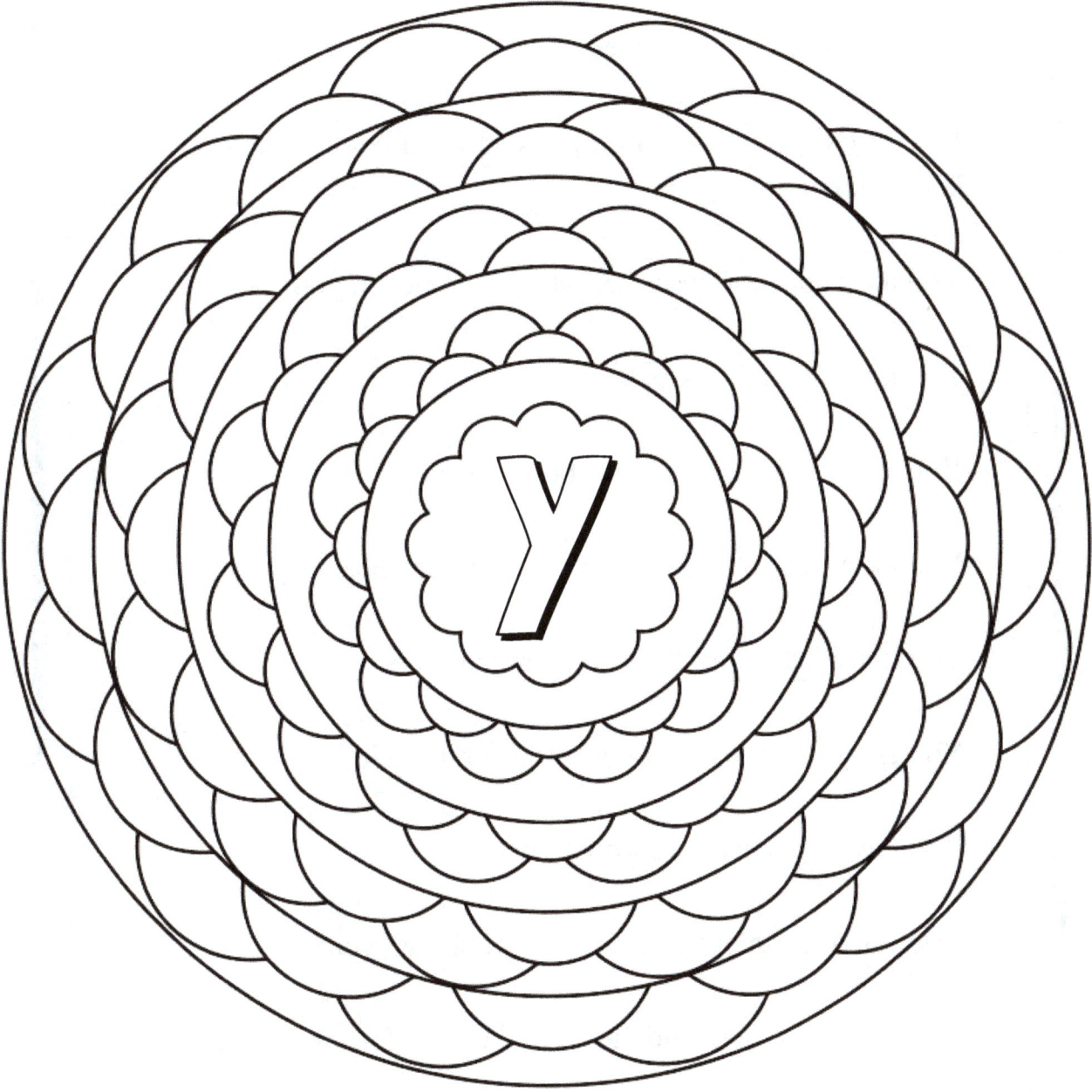

Y is for You

YOU

You are your best promoter.

I tell my clients all the time you can't sell books if no one knows about them.

You are your best promoter when it comes to your book.

You know your book best.

You know what makes your book work.

You know why readers should read your book.

You know where all the good parts are to share.

You should always be the first person to talk your book up.

You have to toot your own horn.

You can tell someone about your book everyday.

You are the person who has to make time for promotion.

Make time and become your best promoter.

YOU CAN DO THIS

Z is for Zeal

ZEAL

Do you have zeal about your book and your book promotion? If you are not excited about your book or your promotion, who else will be?

Write down:

Why did you write this book?

Why do you want to share it with people?

Who do you want to read this book?

Why do you want them to read this book?

HOW TO USE FOR PROMOTION

Write three quotes about why a reader should read your book.

Share the quotes as a graphic or post.

_____

_____

_____

_____

NOTES

_____

_____

_____

_____

_____

_____

_____

_____

_____

NOTES

_____

_____

_____

_____

_____

_____

_____

_____

_____

NOTES

**Join my mailing list for
monthly coloring sheets
and updates on upcoming books
http://bit.ly/LCHColoring**

HOFFMAN
CONTENT, LLC

lashaundahoffman.com

www.ingramcontent.com/pod-product-compliance
Lightning Source LLC
Chambersburg PA
CBHW081523040426
42447CB00013B/3319